Cover image

Painting - oil on burlap - by Giambattista della Rovere ("Il Fiamminghino)

Galleria Sabauda - Turin

Guido Pagliarino

THE MYSTERIOUS

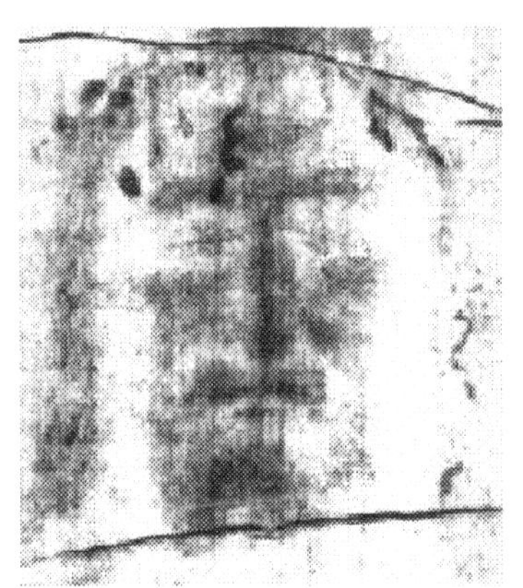

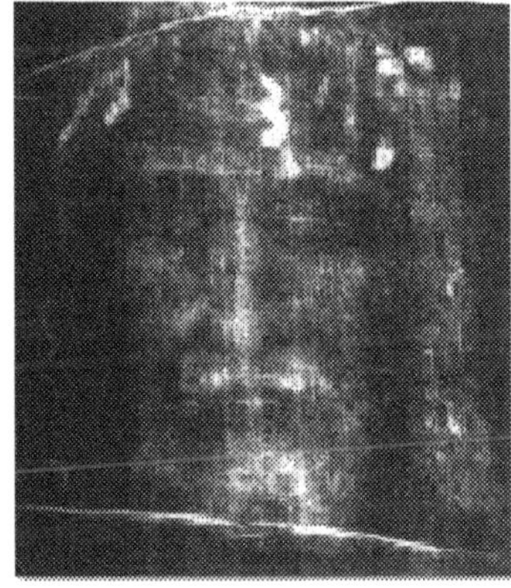

SHROUD OF TURIN

Essay

Guido Pagliarino

THE MYSTERIOUS

SHROUD OF TURIN

a translation into International English from the Italian essay *La misteriosa Sindone di Torino*

The first edition of this essay was published in HTML, by the Author, on his Web site in August 2000

LULU PRESS

Lulu Enterprises, Inc.

860 Aviation Parkway, Suite 300 Morrisville

NC 27560

U.S.A.

First edition

October 2006

ISBN-10: 1-84753-821-5

ISBN-13: 978-1-84753-821-5

A VERY SHORT INTRODUCTION BY THE AUTHOR

I'm a Christian but my Faith is not based on the Shroud of Turin: it's based, directly, on Christ's Resurrection testified by the Apostles; therefore, this essay essentially has the modest purpose to introduce and examine the Shroud and it does not want to induce the reader to believe to think that the Sheet has wrapped Christ's body or, as commonly said, that it's authentic; however, I suppose that the affirmative reasons are prevailing: many are the data in favor and only two facts are against and just one of them is objectively considerable: the tests of the carbon 14; however, many experts say that these tests were not convincing; the other adverse reason is the anticlerical prejudice: it's very strong and leads to consider with nuisance the Shroud without investigating enough the matter.

I thank Miss Gloria Filippi for her precious suggestions about the translation from Italian into English.

Turin, October 19th, 2006

Guido Pagliarino

A) In synthesis:

THE MYSTERIOUS

SHROUD OF TURIN

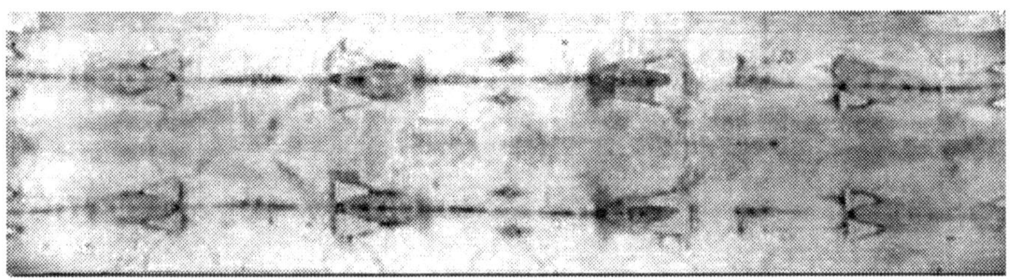

The Shroud of Turin before June 20th, 2002

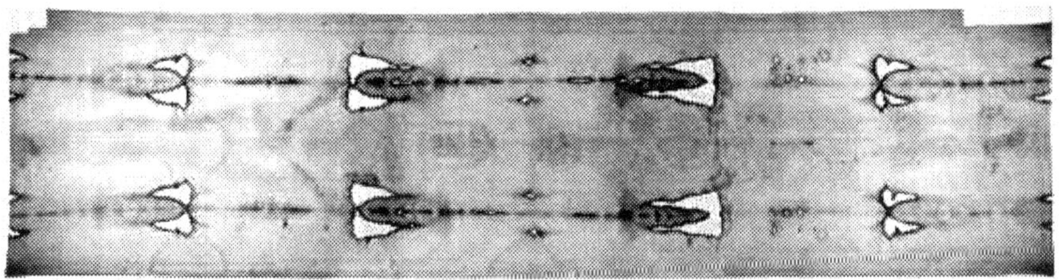

The Shroud of Turin after July 22nd, 2002: during the days from June 20th to July 22nd., 2002, patchs and also Holland lining sewed on its back were taken

– Arcidiocesi di Torino photo, for The Press -

The Turin Shroud (***Sindòn*** in the Gospels' ancient Greek language: it means a funeral cloth, a sheet made of linen and, generally, a sheet, a piece of cloth) - *The* Holy Shroud for Catholics - is a ***flax piece of cloth*** made by a technique ("*thorn of fish*") in use from five thousand to two thousand years ago in Egypt, in Palestine and in other zones of the Middle East. The spinning is "like Z", skewed in sense time, rather than the spinning instead in successive ages "like S", in anticlockwise sense. They are techniques of spinning and weaving of which the Middle Ages have already lost memory. This sheet measures 4,37 meters in length and 1,11 in width.

The Turin Archbishop *pro tempore* (the archbishop who sits at a certain moment on the Episcopal desk of Turin) is the official caretaker of the Shroud.

Shroud has been in Turin since 1578, with a few occasional absences, usually for wars, as during the French siege at the town of 1706 and, the last time, during the II worldwide conflict: in 1939 (in forecast also Italy, as it happened in 1940, will enter into war) it was moved, in order to repair it from the bombardments, into the Montevergine Sanctuary, near Avellino. It got back in Turin in 1946.

Shroud of Turin, but all people say simply "*the* Shroud", is still, partially, a ***mysterious*** sheet.

It can be observed also by the photo: on the Shroud there are various spots, whose nature and cause partially, not entirely, are notes. As we will see, for a part of these spots the Shroud is like a negative film. On the contrary, for other ones, not: they are positive.

Without doubt...

On this sheet, we find some patches and some signs of burns.

It's sure, by the analyses of experts, invisible deposits of pollens from vegetation of the Middle East, and pollens from flora of the Alps are on the Shroud; moreover, traces of aloe and myrrh; and of aragonite (it's a calcium carbonate, iron and strontium composition), an earth in Jerusalem and, in particular, in a tomb studied by Prof. Levy-Setti, from Chicago: he, confronting with the aragonite on the Shroud, has concluded that the two earths are exactly equal.

It's moreover sure, by analysis made by various pathologists of international reputation, between them we find Prof. Luigi Baima Bollone from Turin, spots of coagulated blood, group AB, male DNA, are on the Shroud

Sudario - shroud - of Oviedo

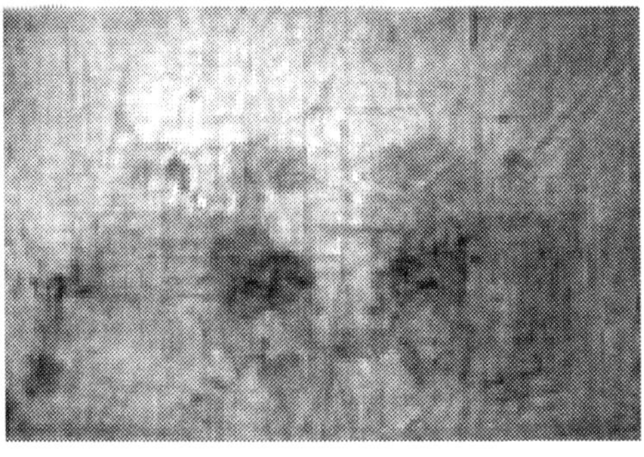

It's curious to know that blood of identical type AB, male, is on *the Sudario* - shroud - *of Oviedo* (Spain), one burlap 83x52 centimeters large – Is it the *true* Veronica's Handkerchief ?! It may be, but in Rome we find another Veronica's holy relic (?) –. These haematic impressions are in symmetrical shapes and recall, in the complex, a human face. Moreover, it's also interesting the following fact about the rests (holy relics) of the miracle (we know by the tradition) happened in the VIIIth century in Lanciano in province of Chieti, Italy (a clergyman had doubted of the presence of Christ in the Eucharist, while he was consecrating, and the bread and the wine were transformed in meat and blood); they are 1) coagulated blood, group AB like the one on the Shroud of Turin; 2) human meat of myocardium: analysis was made in 1970 by Prof. Odoardo Linoli, pathologist. I do not know if the Lanciano Sanctuary manages a Web site.

Lanciano Sanctuary, holy relics

On the Shroud of Turin, we find some spots of blood with separate blood serum (it means corpse blood) and some other spots without separation: the last ones come from a person still alive.

It's certain that the cloth has endured burns, by a first fire in a far past time. Most obvious signs of a second one remain: on December 4, 1532, the Shroud chapel in Chambery, Savoy, France, where the sheet was kept, flared up; we may see two burned lines for all the length of the sheet; the Shroud suffered also holes, along these burned lines, but the holes was covered, by patches, by Clare's nuns of a close convent; moreover these nuns sewed, in order to reinforce the sheet, one Holland lining on its back, along all its extension.

It is of all obvious that on this piece of cloth, the images forehead and back of a human body are impressed.

The human image impressed on the Shroud is like one of a negative film. Therefore, impressed photographically on a film, or more anciently on a negative slab, it appears positive as if the Man had been reflected and into this mirror-Shroud his image had been photographed: therefore, as in every negative and for an image into the mirror, what is left appears like right and, on the contrary, the right appears like the left.

In the next page we may see the positive and the negative of a photo of a Byzantine icon and soon, under, we may see the positive and the negative of a photo of the face of the Shroud Man.

Photography of an icon - a human work -

Negative of the same photo

Photography of the Shroud Face

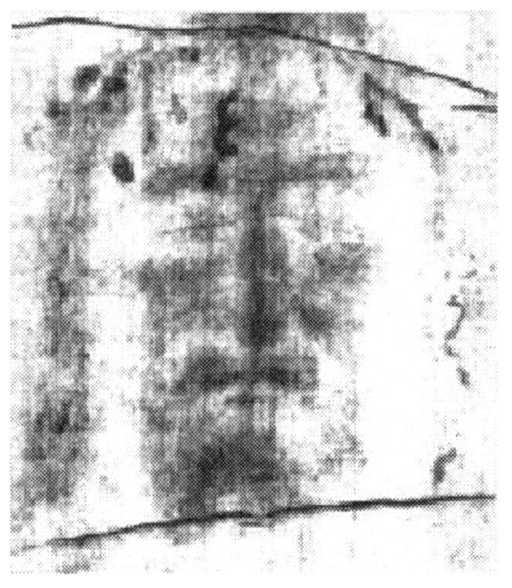

Negative of the same photo

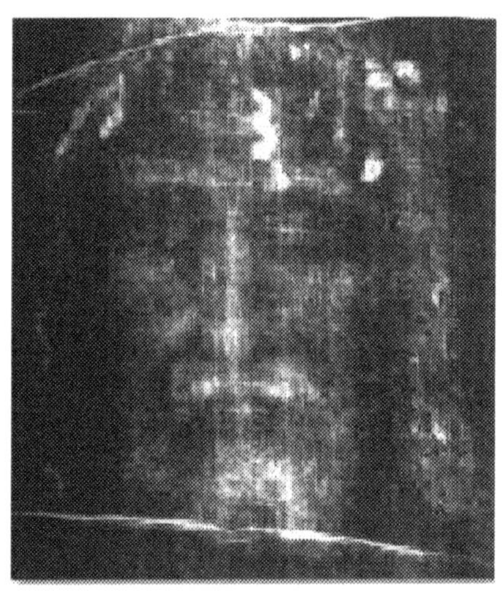

Those lines that cross hair and beard are two folds of the sheet due to unknown causes; they and the blood spots (as an example, the one, much obvious, on the forehead that has the shape, respective, of a 3 turned upside down on the image to right and of a 3 on that one on the left) on the contrary of the face turn out positive in the right photo and turn out negative in the left one.

We know this sheet (*sindòn*) is of the same type used in order to wrap corpses in Palestine at the century of Jesus, even if it was in use, in alternative, wrapping about the dead body bandages like the Egyptians, what we know, also, by the John's Gospel about the corpse of Lazarus from Betània. The dead body was stretched supine on the sheet, with the feet at extremity and with the head towards center of the cloth (to times, on the contrary: the head towards end and the feet towards the center); the other half of the sheet was withdrawn on the corpse that, therefore, remained comprised within the *sindòn.*

In section:

Shroud --

[feet] corpse [head]] Shroud

Shroud--

Sheet or bandages?

Only Matthew, Mark and Luke, writing about the interment of Jesus, say he was placed in *sindòn*, in a sheet. John do not write about a *sindòn* (shroud). He talks on the finding of the funeral flaxes of Jesus, the morning of the next Sunday after the Friday of the crucifixion, in the Christ's empty grave: in many translations from ancient Greek into Italian, we find bende (bandages), instead lenzuolo or sindone (sheet).

If one reads the term **in ancient Greek**, knows that Peter and John found[1] ***othònia*** and this word means ***flax fabrics***, at the plural in ancient Greek. Therefore, they was not ***bandages*** like we find in some translation. Because the term ***othònia*** means generic flax woven, this word can mean, being ***plural*** word, **also** a sheet between other recovered fabrics; sure it does not mean bandages. The other three Gospels Authors do not tell us the Jesus' Shroud was compound by flax: John wrote after, between the years 90 and 100, and he wanted *overwhelm the gap.* If John would have spoken about **bandages**, he would have used not **othònia** but **keirìai** (bandages), like we read for revived Lazarus, in the same Book (11 - 44).

---

[1] …and recovered them? Or was the owner of the grave, Joseph from Arimatea, to recover them?)

About the history of the Shroud

The history of the Shroud from the years 1353-6 is documented without empty periods of time[2]. In the previous centuries, we find above all hypothesis and tradition and very few documents. There is an historical empty space between the year of the crucifixion of Jesus (30 - 33) and the VIth century and there is a nearly empty space from the Costantinopoli's conquest, by the crusaders in the year 1204, to the years 1353 - 1356:

Only a single document, precisely a nearly document, composed in this period has been found: a miniature in **the Pray Code**. This religious code is today, since few years, in Prague; it was composed between the years 1192 - 95, obviously by hand, because it was long time before the discovery in the West World of printing. This miniature represents the Christ's deposition: Jesus do not show the thumbs, they are withdrawn under the palms of the hands; and the same thing we find for the Man on the Shroud of Turin (and we will see because); and like on the Shroud, this miniature represents one of the legs laiding upon the second leg. Moreover, on a sheet painted in the miniature, we may see little circles disposed in a group of a similar shape to one of the four groups, everyone composed by four burned holes that we find on the Shroud of Turin. Truly, on this Shroud they are between some very little circles; however, those large ones immediately appear to the eyes:

---

[2] See: Appendix 1, Chronology.

down below, you may see the photo of one of those groups. The four symmetrical groups of holes are, approximately, in the center of the four rectangles deriving from folding the sheet in four parts. Evidently, when those holes were produced by burn, the Shroud was refolded in four and this fact provoked the lesions passed to all the four layers. The reason of these burns is unknown, but it's known that they are in the cloth before 1532, the year of the fire of the Shroud Chapel in Chambery: these lesions are in fact reproduced on a previous etching attributed to Dürer, realized in the same Chambery in 1516, which reproduces on the Shroud the four symmetrical groups of holes. The author of the miniature of the Pray Code affirms in the text that he was inspired from a shroud. We may suppose he saw the same is conserved today in Turin; and we may suppose the first fire was previous the date of composition of the Pray Code.

[Bullets indicate the groups]

O O

O O

Pray Code

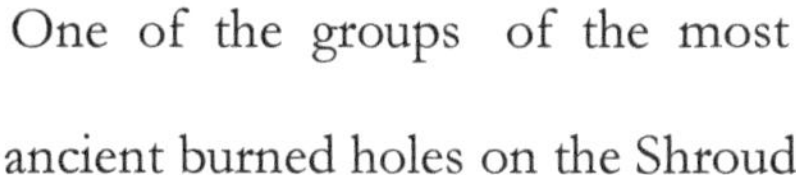

One of the groups of the most ancient burned holes on the Shroud

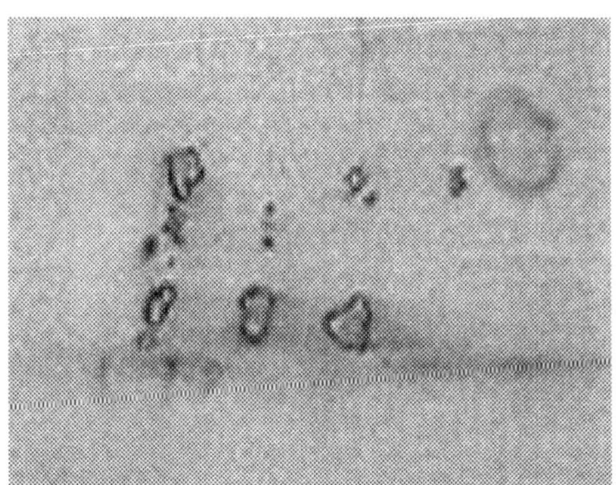

Magnified particular with evidenced holes

Evidenced four holes' groups on the Shroud of Turin -particular -

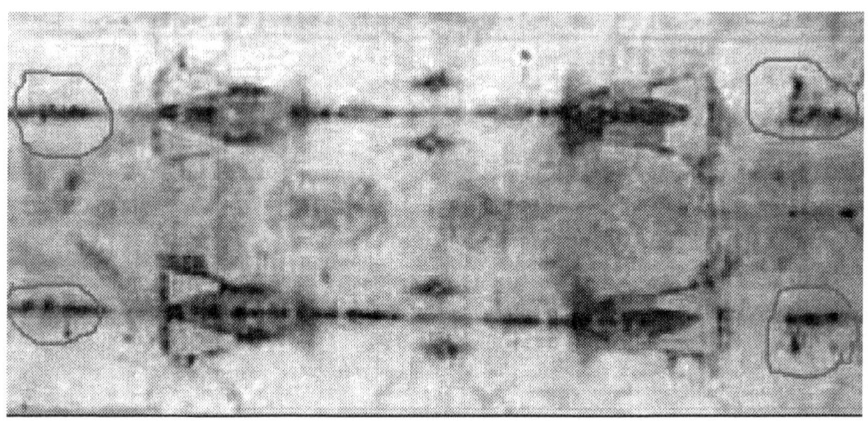

But... what about the following fact?

The age of birth of the Shroud has been fixed, by three laboratories, "between years 1260 and 1390", approximately one/two centuries after the Pray Code. Being authorized from the Church, in 1988 these laboratories took champions from the Shroud and in order to establish its seniority they have subjected them to experiments based on radioactive carbon 14; but only one of the two possible methods was employed: instead, it would have been necessary to use them both, in order to be sure. However, several times the two methods presented absurdities about the results. For example, shells of alive snails were dated at 26.000 years ago. A Viking horn of the 1000 was dated at the XXI century (!). The Lindow Man was dated, on three samples of its, first time at

300 B.C., second time at the I century A.D. and third time, at the century V, with a discard of 800 years. About bones and bandages of the same Egyptian mummy, preserved in the Museum Of Manchester, the first sample turned out to be older of 1000 years than the second one, while they are contemporary. Here, in this synthesis, I only add that, from great time, for many reasons, the result of those analyses on the Shroud is rejected from many scientists, some Christian and some not Christian. Between these scientists, we find the great searchers Prof. Garza Valdés, Prof. Moroni, Prof. Bettinelli, Prof. Barbesino and Prof. Koutznezov.

About the human *image* on the Shroud

According to the analyses of all the experts that studied the Shroud, between the others, Alan Adler, professor of chemistry in the Western Connecticut State University, the human figure isn't produced according to known methods. It's not fruit of a painting, there are not traces of colors: there are not pigments, neither pastes nor colorful powders. The image is not produced by press, inks are not been found.

The image is not even made by singeing the Shroud (approximately it is as it happens when an ignited iron is forgotten over a shirt and a burnt print remains on); this means it's not originated from the contact with a overheated metal relief, because the image by singeing passes from one part to the other part. Image of the Shroud Man is instead most superficial.

The image moreover remains deformed, because the cloth is in contact with a relief, three dimensions, for which the burnt print appearing on the surface of the fabric, two dimensions, is wider of the real one. This is not true for the Shroud: the image is not deformed.

A burnt image has different fluorescence in comparison to the image of the Shroud, and it does not have three-dimensional base; instead, from the Shroud, we could obtain **holographic photos of the Man**: the first time, in 1977, in USA by Eric J. Jumper and John P. Jackson.

The photographic 3D – three dimensions – is possible if the light received from the object is to different distances from the various parts of the same object. Suppose a luminous source placed in a point of the space, like a lamp: its light must cover less distance in order to reach the nose that is more prominent, and a longer way to reach the mouth, because it's less prominent.

The photo of a painting or, generally, of a bi-dimensional figure cannot turn out three-dimensional, because all its points are on the same plan, at the same distance from the lighting source. This fact demonstrates that the Man of the Shroud is not simple image but something more.

In 1978, a three-dimensional photo of the Face was realized in Turin, Italy, from the team of Prof. Tamburelli.

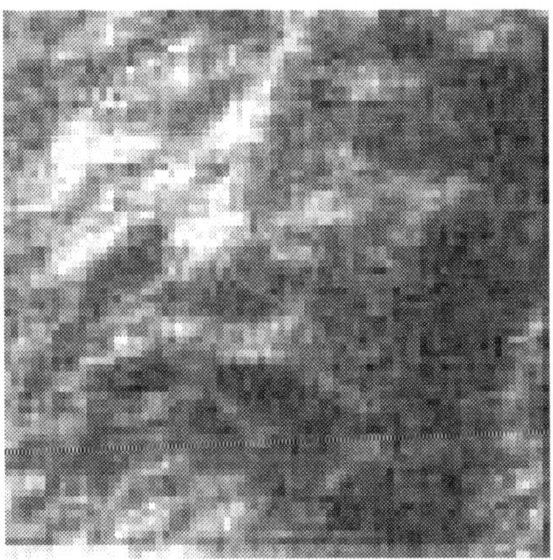

By electronic procedures cleaning the image of the photography of the Man of the Shroud, without artful manoeuvre and extraneous information, independently from the Americans, the team of professor Tamburelli has reached finally the following holographic image:

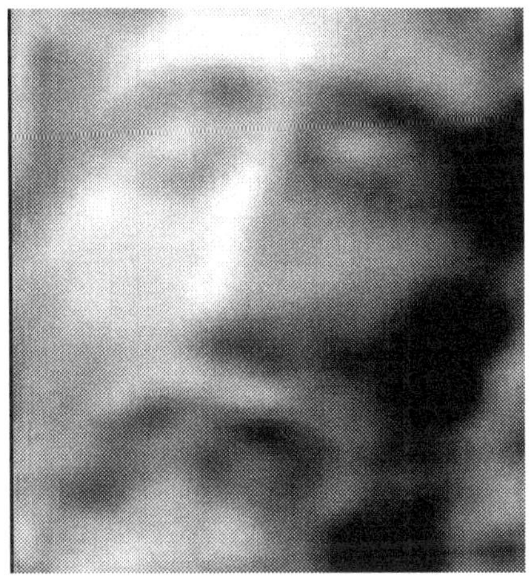

Then, Prof. Tamburelli and Prof. Balossino have compared the obtained face with those of icons painted between VIth century and the XIIth: they have turned out to correspond to the face of the Shroud for beyond 100 points (according to a particular mathematical calculation), more than are required (minimum 60 points) to consider two faces as those of the same person. The common features confirm the uniqueness of such Jesus's image and they make more probable as much as already to naked eye one may guess: the face of the Shroud had been the prototype of those icons.

Icon of Christ Pantocrator (please, compare it with the face obtained by Prof. Tamburelli)

Why the Shroud Man's thumbs are not visible and why his right foot covers the other one?

Two nails (used to fix every arm to the cross) enter into the *Space of Destot* in correspondence of the *carpus* (wrist-joint) and pierce and damage the median nerves; this action causes the reflexing of the thumb under the palm of the hand (Prof. Barbet). These things were not known in the Middle Ages, in which people thought the nails pierced hands, not wrists. We have to suppose (?) the presumed medieval forger of the Shroud knew them between 1260 and 1390 ! Looking on the Shroud, we see the two wounds by nails in the superior limbs of the Man are in the wrists and are not in the hands, and these have invisible thumbs, withdrawn behind the palms: by lesion of the median nerves.

The left foot is nailed on the right one by one nail, therefore a leg of the man is bent. When the death arrives, by the *rigor mortis* the first leg remains bent, how it was on the cross, with the left foot positioned over the other one: in the negative photo of the sheet; on the contrary, on the Shroud or in its positive photo the right foot is over the left one.

Coins

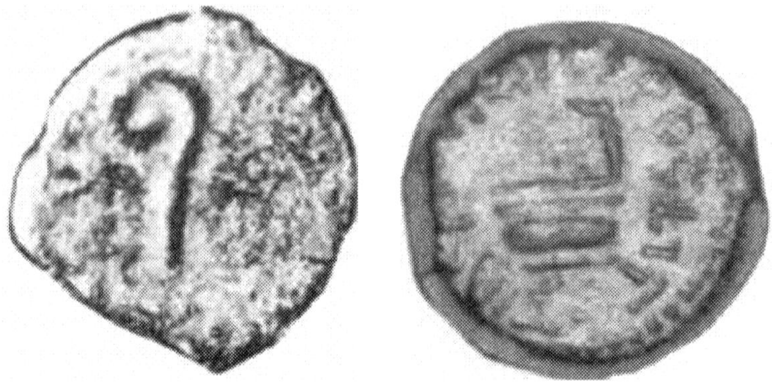

On the ocular orbits of the Face of the Shroud the marks of two Roman coins have been identified. These coins have the inscription, in ancient Greek, "Tiberius Caesar" and also the image of a sacred ladle. The first mark was found out in 1954 by Father F.L. Filas, on the eyelid of the right eye. An expert, the numismatic M. Marx identified it like the mark of a coin executed by Pontius Pilatus between the years 29 and 32 (A.D.). Prof. Tamburelli, by the help of a computer, has confirmed these studies. Prof. Baima Bollone and Prof. Balossino have interpreted a few signs on the left eyebrow arch as owed another coin presumedly of the same Roman epoch.

The use of placing a coin on each closed eye of corpses had the purpose to have not them reopened by the possible mechanical contractions during the period immediately following the death.

Aloe and myrrh

Aloe and myrrh found on the Shroud correspond to the aromas which the Gospels tell us, used to grease Jesus's body before the burial. We read in the Gospels that for the haste, Jesus's corpse was not washed but only greased, because it was nearly Saturday, the sacred rest's day for the Hebrews. Otherwise, on the Shroud it should not have remained any blood track.

Crurifragium

The convicts were on the cross for a long period of time, to the still alive ones the legs were broken (Roman *Crurifragium*), since they could not any more lean on the foot-rest if they had been tied, or on the nail, avoiding so, temporarily, the asphyxia which crops out when a person is hung up; therefore their death allowed the end of the guard service. Gospels tell us the Christ's legs were not broken because soldiers saw he was dead (however, for security, one of them pierced by a lance his heart). The legs are in fact whole on the Shroud; and there is the very clear sign of a lance blow and remains of corpse blood (blood and *water*) gone out.

Signs of wounds and of abrasions

We find on the Shroud all the lesions Jesus suffered during his passion and death, how the Gospels refer. Looking the Shroud photographic slab, we may see what follows (on the Shroud - like a negative film - what is "at right" is, in the reality, and on the negative photographic slab, "at left"; and on the contrary, what is "at left" is in the reality, "at right").

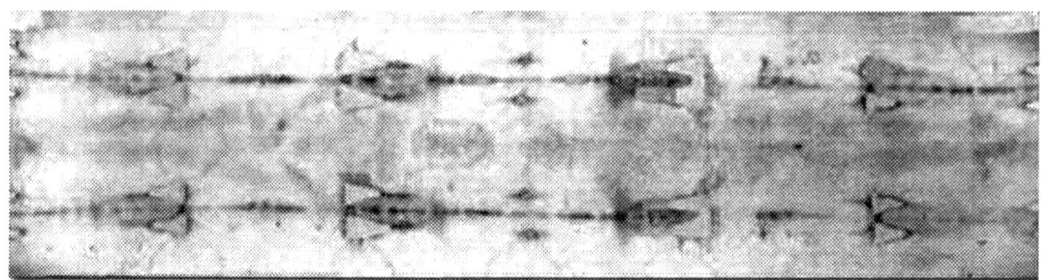

Observing the photographic slab and seeing the image from the beginning of the sheet and after proceeding up to his half, we may see (it's confirmed by all the experiments of the pathologists that have studied the Shroud):

- Wounded by nail at the left foot *(the right one is covered from the first; in fact, we know the feet were nailed to the vertical pole of the cross with an only nail and, after the death, they stayed in the same position, for the rigor mortis: on the Shroud (and on the contrary on the slab) the right foot and the left one appear respectively as the left foot and the right one, because - it was said to satiety - the Shroud image is a negative specular image).*

- Wound by nail on the right wrist (*the left one is covered by the right wrist, because the hands are crossed in such position to cover the pubic zone).*

- Wound by lance to the chest, up to the heart, with sign of a big blood flow which drips from the wound along the chest and the side.

- Wounds on the forehead, produced by plugs: one of them is very deep, from which a blood flow at form of a 3 has gone out.

Seeing from the center of the sheet and proceeding toward our right, we may find:

- Wounds by plugs on the nape *(in total, these wounds by plugs are more than 30).*

- Abrasions on the back, under the shoulders, caused by the transport of a heavy beam (*patibulum* of the cross)

- More than 120 wounds produced by a Roman scourge, on the back, gluteus, legs and heels.

- The bleeding right heel; the bleeding left foot (precisely, under).

Statistics

Taking into consideration all the known data on the Shroud, mathematicians and statistical researchers, independently one from the others, have calculated there is only a possibility against millions (for someone, against billions) this sheet has not wrapped the corpse of Jesus and the man's image is not that of Christ. According to Father Filas, 1 possibility is existing against 10 followed from 26 zeros possibilities the man who was in the Shroud was not Jesus from Nazareth. For the researcher Donovan, who afterwards calculated with a more prudent method, there is a possibility against 225 billions.

For the researchers Stevensen and Habermas (they have wanted to do a calculation absolutely for fault) there is one possibility against 82,944,000. Prof. Fanti and Prof. Marinelli have arrived to conclude that the probability the image is not of Christ is one against many millions. Therefore, it tends to the certainty, statistically, the Shroud of Turin has really wrapped the dead body of Jesus and the image is that of Christ

Negative photos of right half and left half of the Shroud, printed on cloth at natural size. During the Oxtension in the year 2000 of the Original, they was exposed in the chapel of the San Lorenzo church, near the Cathedral, in which the Original was lodged the first time, just after its arrival in Turin from Chambery.

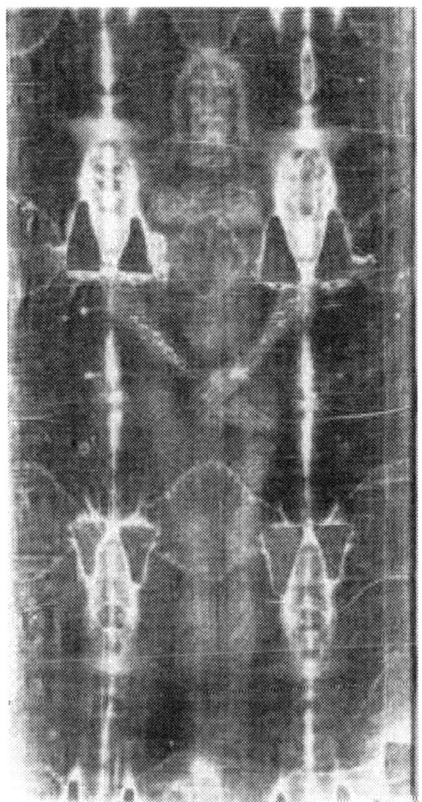

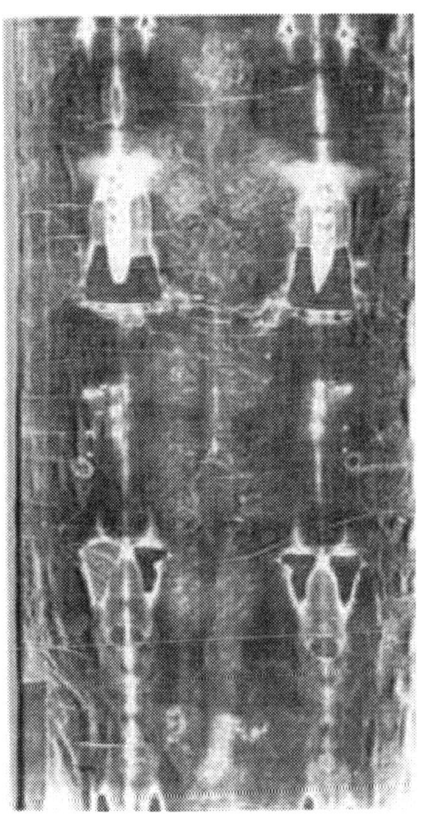

B) In particular:

I
THE PHOTOGRAPHIES

Secondo Pia's camera: it's conserved in the Shroud Museum of Turin

In 1898, in occasion of the marriage of Prince Vittorio Emanuele, heir to the throne of Italy, there is a Shroud Oxtension. Father Natale Noguier de Malijay, Salesian priest, would like the Sheet photographed for the first time. He ask Baron Manno to obtain a royal permission, because this noble lives near the throne and he can convince the King Umberto to give his assent: the King is the Shroud owner. The authorization is given, but, for formal reasons, the initiative shouldn't appear official, the task is not entrusted to a professional photographer, but to a famous lawyer of Turin, Mr Secondo Pia. This person is a friend of Baron Manno and also president of a club of amateur photographers, he is a good photographer; and, not less important, he is a member of the commission for the Exposure of Sacred Art which took place in Turin in the same period of the Oxtension.

The first photographic click happens on 25 May 1898, but this attempt of Mr Pia fails. On 28 May, he makes new photos, with the aid of an adjuvant of him, Mr Sartore, and of another amateur of the club, Lieutenant Fino. By his own machine, Father Maria Sanna Solaro takes other photos. After the development, this lawyer sees the negative of the image of the Shroud; this negative photo represents, in truth, a figure in positive. Mr Pia begins to shake and nearly the slab falls to him. Anticlericals accuse him to have operated makes up, but the spreading of the providential photos of Father Sanna Solaro this priest had held for himself removes the controversies. In the year 1931, in order to conclude the public celebrations for the wedding of the future "King of May" Umberto II with Princess Mary José of Belgium, a new Oxtension of the Shroud take place. This time, a famous professional photographer, Giuseppe Enrie, receives the task to photograph the Shroud. He is helped from the still alive lawyer Mr Pia and from a Salesian, professor Tonelli. Many photos are made, in inner and in exteriors: three of the whole Shroud and nine of details, between which the Face of the Man. It is repeated totally, even better, what was already uncovered. Various doctors, first one professor Pierre Barbet, helped by these photos, begins to take care of the Shroud. It is repeated totally, even better, what was already uncovered. Prof.

Barbet, observing the numerous hurts on the Shroud Man, asserts without doubt it's the image of a person flagellated and crucifix. He declares the thumbs are not lookable because automatically they have been refolded under the palm of the respective hands, for the lesion of the nerves caused from the nails planted in the wrists, nails which are passed into the anatomical "Space of Destot".

In 1969, during a recognition of the archbishop of Turin cardinal Pellegrino in order to assess the state of the Shroud, it is the time of the color photographies. The professional photographer Giovanni Battista Judica Cordiglia is charged to click. He releases coloured photographies and photographies in black and white, of the entire figure and all its details: on ordinary light, infrared beams, ultraviolet, Wood's light.

In 1977, in Houston, John Jackson and Eric Jumper made three-dimensional elaborations, by computer. Realized independently in 1978, the best ones was made by Giovanni Tamburelli of Turin, in collaboration with Nello Balossino.

In other words, the interest of scientists in the Shroud of Turin started with the first photographies of Mr. Pia.

II

THE SEARCH ON THE SHROUD BEGINS

Since the year 1932, Dr. Pierre Barbet and other physicians (interested to the old photographies and to the new ones made by Mr. Enrie) begin to take care of the Shroud . Dr. Barbet asserts that the many wounds on the body of the Man demonstrate that the Shroud has wrapped the corpse of a person flagellated and crucifix, and that the invisible thumb of his hand (like if it was withdrawn behind the palm) is consequence reflected of a nail in the wrist and of its passage through the anatomical "space of Destot". Some theories are formulated on the modalities of formation of the image. Already in 1901 Paul Vignon (considering that the figure of the Shroud is in negative) had introduced his "steam graphical" theory: the figure would have been impressed "photographically", he asserted, for natural chemical reaction between the aloe and myrrh and ammoniacal cloth and vapors emanating from the dead body. The same theory (with some variations) is adjusted from other researchers (Judica Cordiglia – not the photographer –, Moroni, Romanese, Intrigillo, Rodante) after the year 1932, in consequence of new recognitions on the photos and, but not close to the cloth exposed. Only during the Shroud Oxtension of the year 1978, inspections directly on the cloth are finally granted. The scientists discover, then, that the image derives from one modification of superficial fibers of the cellulose of the flax of the linen. They do not succeed to discover the relative cause. Some characteristics remain not reproduceable. The "steam graphical" theory is abandoned from the 1978.

In the years 1973 and 1978, the Swiss biologist Max Frej Sulzer, also criminologist, university teacher and consultant of the police, carries out with adhesive tapes withdrawals of powders deposits on the Shroud. He finds micro traces which, under the microscope, after several analysis, reveal that themselves are microscopical fossil grains of pollen of plants growing only in Anatolia and Palestine; he goes in those places in order to carry out comparisons with alive pollens of the local flora; moreover, he recovers pollens of plants of alpine flora which grows, among other things, in the zone of Chambery. He also finds, being astonished, rice pollens: someone will remember that the Shroud had been exposed, in the past time, also near Vercelli, a land where the rice is cultivated. The kinds of pollen correspond to the migrations of the Shroud according to the tradition and, after, to the history. In the year 1977 the Americans John Jackson and Eric Jumper (members of the STURP: Shroud of Turin Research Project) submit a few photographies of the Shroud to electronic elaboration and they discover the three dimensions of these photos, 3 D not possessed from normal photographies and, generally, from icons produced from the human being. The year after, Prof. Giovanni Tamburelli, of Turin, independently, obtains better three-dimensional images. He finds confirmation of a circular print on the right eyelid discovered from Francis Filas in the year 1954, due, he supposes with probability, to a known coin, coined under Ponzio Pilato in the year 29. Later on, with Nello Balossino, Giovanni Tamburelli executes another elaboration which conduces to a Face cleaned from the wounds and filterings of blood. Later on, Nello Balossino and Pierluigi Baima Bollone interpret signs found on the arcade of the left eyebrow of the Face, like traces of a second coin. In the same time, Balossino and Tamburelli compare the images they obtained by electronic elaborations, with many icons representing the face of Jesus (VI - XIII century); they use a method of superimposition and mathematical elaboration: : with an index of probability very high, the features of the faces are common. A strong hypothesis can be drawn: those icons were inspired to the Shroud face. In the year 1978, Pierluigi Baima Bollone (Legal Medicine professor at the University of Turin and also a consultant of the Legal Court of Turin and the director of the "Shroud of Turin International Center of Studies") stamp takes threads from the so-called haematic zones of the Sheet; during the years, he carries out various examinations, concluding that on the Shroud there are traces of human blood, group AB; partially, he asserts, the traces have the characteristics of red globules. Other traces found by Prof. Baima Bollone are constituted of residuals of aloe and myrrh. At the same time but indipendently, the American group of research STURP verifies the presence of the blood. Besides, through fluorescence examinations and the spectroscopy and the reflected light, it establish the total absence on the Shroud of colored pigments. Alan Adler, university professor of chemistry at the "Connecticut Western Been University", carry out an analysis on a champion, and he arrives to the exclusion that the Shroud image is a painting. The April 21 1988, having the authorization of the caretaker of the Shroud, the Archbishop of Turin Cardinal Ballestrero, from the advanced part of the Shroud (corner to the left of who watches) three champions of woven are captures; they are exposed to radiometric dating, according to the method of radiocarbon (the C14), from the laboratories of Oxford, Zurich and Tucson. These experiments establish that the age of the Shroud is comprised between the 1260 and the 1390. The Cardinal Ballestrero, diligently, provides this result immediately in a public declaration, showing to accept it without reserves. It results a great disappointment between the supporters of the Shroud like a relic. On the contrary, it results a great satisfaction between the Protestants because enemies of the sacred images and the veneration of the relics. The experiments get also a big satisfaction for Anticlericals. However, many scientists begin soon to have doubts about the value of the result; the search about the possibility of a correct and serious dating of the Shroud woven is now in a phase of study and comparison.

It interests also the science the system of conservation of the cloth, because the Shroud is subject to deterioration. In the year 1992 an experts commission was instituted by the new caretaker and Archbishop of Turin, Cardinal Saldarini, because they verify the conditions of the Shroud and propose the necessary interventions for a good conservation of it in the future. In the year 1996 the commission establishes that, for the future, the Shroud must remain always unfolded: it, during many centuries and until then it has been rolled up around a cylinder between an Oxtension and another, and before than it was conserved withdrawn in eight parts. The Shroud is therefore extended in one glass (protected from bullets) theca dipped in inert gas, like a watertight compartment, protected from the influence of the light. This system is inaugurated during the Oxtension of 1998. In June 2000, it comes completed, for the Oxtension of the same year, a second container which continues to guard *the Cloth.* For the generation and the monitoring of the inner gaseous atmosphere, the same system used for the Oxtension is employed (with minimal modifications). The Shroud has been withdrawn in suitable niche, in its turn structured for the best possible conservation, in the chapel under the Royal Platform, in the cathedral.

The new theca and the relative flowing support have been realized the first from the Alenia Aerospazio and the second from the Microtecnica, using the most advanced aerospace technologies. The theca and the support have been obtained, by milling, from a monolithic aeronautical aluminum alloy block. The container guarantees perfect watertight estate; it's connected to a system of bellows of compensation in stainless steel containing, at the lowest degree, the internal over-pressure regarding the outside environment in case of varying of the atmospheric conditions.

III

THE EXPERIMENTS BY CARBON 14

Upon what principle is based the *radiometric dating by the Carbon 14 (C14)*

Every living vegetable breathes carbon dioxide, which is composed of oxygen and carbon. A minimal part of this last one is radioactive (C 14), while the greatest part (C 12) don't. Therefore all the living plants incorporate radioactive carbon. The animals, and the man, feeding themselves of vegetables (and also eating other animals having eaten vegetables) assume C 14. When a vegetable and an animal are dead, the radioactive carbon which impregnates them diminishes, always more with the passing of the time. The same, about those objects deriving from the living beings, as, for example, weaved wool of sheep, from the moment in which the sheep is sheared and, therefore, the wool, separated from the animal, dies. 5730 years are necessary in average so that C 14 which is present in a dead creature, or in an object from it derived, is halved, 11,460 because it's reduced to a quarter, 17,200 to an eighth. Establishing, by two methods, and very complicated calculations, how much C 14 remains at the moment of the experiment, a person can know the seniority of the champion subordinated to radiometric dating.

The first, not very known and unofficial, experiment, by the method of the C14, of dating of a Shroud champion

In occasion of the television Oxtension in the year 1973, a small part of the Shroud is taken; it reaches Dr. Raes, who takes advantage in order to try to establish its age. He carries out two disappointing tests, with the two halves of the scrap in his possession: the first turns out dated II century and the second X century. A result without meant.

The official experiments of radiometric dating of the year 1988: because they are not totally acceptable.

Some ones, like the philosopher Gianni Vattimo in an article on La Stampa of the August 17, 2000, thinks that they prevail the reasons in order to consider the Shroud an object of age later than the time of Jesus. If they are excluded the *radiometric dating* tests of 1988, establishing a seniority within the years 1260 and 1390, all the interdisciplinary researches (Anatomy, Biology, Legal Medicine, Anthropology, Archaeology, Biblical studies, History, Photography in two and three dimensions, Electronics, Computer science, Study of the fossil pollens, Physics, Chemistry, History of the art) conduce to another conclusion. One may consider, moreover, that the results of the cited radiometric experiment are not considered reliable from many "*carbon 14 men*" like Garza Valdés, Koutznezov and the Italians Mario Moroni, Maurizio Bettinelli and Francisco

Barbesino (but the list of number of researchers – believing and not believing in God – who oppose themselves to the result is longer): the three last scientists carried out some experiments on burlap champions of Egyptian mummies whose seniority was historically famous, having first of all, simulated on them the fire suffered from the Shroud in Chambery in the year 1532. The same author of the two methods of radiometric dating (radiocounts and mass spectrometry), Dr. Libby, one time asserted this kind of dating has its weak point especially in the linen woven; it's possible to add: like the linen of the Shroud. When it comes dealt in order to make spun, the plant of the linen endures the elimination of its lipids and proteins: they are more poor of C 14 than the rest, that rest which will serve to the spinning; therefore, when the spun and the woven are subjects to radiometric dating, they appear much younger than their real age because, in proportion, they have more C 14 of the plant. For having a more precise dating, the researcher would have to be able to work not on the product but on the linen plant from which it was obtained. It's also necessary to know that both methods of dating have carried, many times, to absurd results. As an example, shells of alive snails were aged of 26.000 years ago; a Viking horn certainly of the year 1000 was considered of the XXI century (!); the skin of a mammuth, certainly at least of 25,000 years ago when the species died out, was considered old of 5,600 years only; a seal, just dead, turned out dead 1300 years ago; the Man of Lindow was dated, with 3 samples of his body, once lived in the year 300 a.C. about, a second time of the I century, last time of the Vth century, with a difference of 800 years; bones and bandages of the same Egyptian mummy (this means they were contemporary), conserved at the Museum of Manchester, turned out the first one oldest than 1000 years than the second one; like I said, Shroud spins had been already subordinates unofficially to radiometric dating in the 1973 from Dr. Raes: an extremity of the champion had turned out of the year 200 and the other one of the 1000 A. D.; but in particular, about the official experiments of the year 1988, how the Daily Print wrote, the three interested laboratories did not use both methods, they used only one of them, no laboratory had taken advantage also from the other system, that they would have had to consider scientifically, to resort to both, for control; and the correction factors were not applied, even though the Shroud underwent fires, the most serious one was in Chambery: fires increase the C14 of an object which has endured them, therefore the experiment has the result to make them more recent than they really are; the same thing for the fungi and the bacteria, they absorb C14: after a long period they become chemically arranged to the threads of the Shroud, yielding her their carbon 14, and the effects are not removable by the simple physical cleanness made by the three laboratories, according to how much reported from the mass media: complex chemical procedures are necessary; also the smoke of the candles adds carbon 14, and along centuries many and many candles were ignited in the churches in which the Shroud had been conserved; the same thing one may say for the human touch: the Shroud, during the centuries, had been exposed supported by the hands of clerics and, moreover, it remained for many days in those of the nuns who patched up the holes produced from the fire of the year 1532; also the radioactivity produced from the disaster

of the Soviet atomic central of Cernobyl, April 19, 1986, may have modified the C14 of the Shroud.

Dr. Koutznezov has carried out a test upon a burned woven certainly of the I century, with the correction factors, and he has found the same age, the I century; without these factors, he have found a younger age; therefore, he has risked to assert that the Shroud should be considered made in the I century.

46

IV

WHAT THE SHROUD MEDIEVAL FORGER (AND CYNIC MURDERER) WOULD HAVE TO KNOW AND WOULD HAVE TO MAKE

All scientists who have directly managed the image of the Man of the Shroud think it cannot be produced even today, by moderns means. Sure a counterfeiter who, between 1260 and 1390, would have been able to produce the Shroud would have been a genius greater than Leonardo.

Between bracket: **Leonardo da Vinci** is excluded from our speech on the Shroud whatever somebody may say, in fact he was born (1452) approximately a century after the year 1353 in which the same Shroud was certainly in possession of Geoffrey from Charny; his widow, in 1356, entrusted the Shroud to the canon priests of Lirey, diocese of Troyes: it's sure historically, a report had been wrote and it remains.

Since the experts agree on the fact the Shroud wrapped a human dead body, we understand the counterfeiter would have to procure a corpse murdered by hanging him by nails to a cross, of a man who, alive, had been tortured before in the same way in which Jesus had been: fists; beatings; very strong blow between left eye and nose; flagellation with beyond 120 blows on all the back and on the back of the legs until to the heels; helmet ("crown") of thorns; other lesions to the back due to the weight and the friction of the patibulum of the cross carried from Jesus along the way to the Calvary; abrasions of the skin; therefore, since the counterfeiter could not have found for pure case such dead man, he would have had to make as a prisoner and to torture an alive man and after to kill him on a cross: a sadist murderer, this counterfeiter! After, Jesus was hit into the chest side when he was already a dead man that was done in order to assess if he was dead, like John writes – 19, 34 –, and from the wound, blood and water (today, one says serum) exited, like exactly the blood of a defunct one is, whose two elements decompose themselves after the moment of death, the counterfeiter would have had to transfix the corpse by a nozzle at the just moment, just after the death (not beyond this first moment because the blood would have been clotted): on the Shroud *the blood with its separate serum* leaves from the wound to the chest side and slides along the flank in order to catch up the back of the Man; but

in that time anything was known about the blood liquid and, in particular, nothing was known about the blood circulation (discovered long time after, in the XVII century, by William Harvey who gave public communication of it in 1616), neither it was known that the corpse blood has various different characteristics from that one of an alive person, neither of the difference between venous and arterial blood. The counterfeiter would have (and even today it's impossible according to the experiments of laboratory of

Baima Bollone and of others searchers) to be able to at last remove the body from the sheet without ruining the image, without movements in order not to alter the blood traces on the shape.

Between bracket: only the hypothesis that the material body of Christ was disappeared from the inside of his Shroud and that this sheet became flabby in the same position in which was found lets understand what is the reason of the lacked deformation: in the New Testament, the body of Christ Revived is defined "glorious spiritual"; exactly Paul says that the material animal body is transformed by the Resurrection in glorious spiritual body, and only this transformed body could not deform the prints on the sheet, because the corpse wasn't there anymore. According to some hypotheses, the energy of the Resurrection would have impressed the sheet. Naturally this idea is worth only for the Christian believers; for the others, there is not explanation. It remains the following fact: a counterfeiter removing the corpse would not be successful to not deform the images on the sheet.

That genius criminal would have known many other things. He would have known in advance the principles and the technique of the photography, to be able to produce on the Shroud an image like a photographic negative; and to be able to see the microscopic things, for noticing and then placing on the Shroud the pollens discovered on this sheet and studied in the year 1973 by Max Frey: the microscope was invented centuries after the Middle Ages. Before, he would have had the difficulty to find not whichever pollens but that ones of plants which grow alone in Palestine, Syria and Turkey. He would have had to have at disposition a cloth like one of 2000 years before, woven by the old techniques of that time different from those contemporaries, these last in use already from the end of the Ancient Age / beginning of the Middle Ages; in consequence, the medieval forger (or an accomplice of him) would have had to be able to make a sheet by the technique of spinning and webbing of the I[st] century; however, Middle Ages did not have memory of this technique, so how could he know it: only the recent search discovered it. Besides he would have had to know the crucifixion roman technique: nails in the wrists, not in the hands; but the Middle Ages had lost memory of the crucifixion by the wrists, it has been discovered just in the contemporary age: all the images are not only medieval but still successive, for very long time, those images introduce a Christ nailed by the hands; you just need to visit churches in order to assess it. He would have had to know also the structure of the flagellum, but this structure was not more known in his age in which the penitents who was called "the flagellating" used instruments deprived of the hooks or the two metallic little ball united like a handle-bar, the ones or the others placed in the roman flagellum at the extremities of the ropes united to the manic, which of usual was at least three and not two like in the submitted image. Moreover the counterfeiter would have

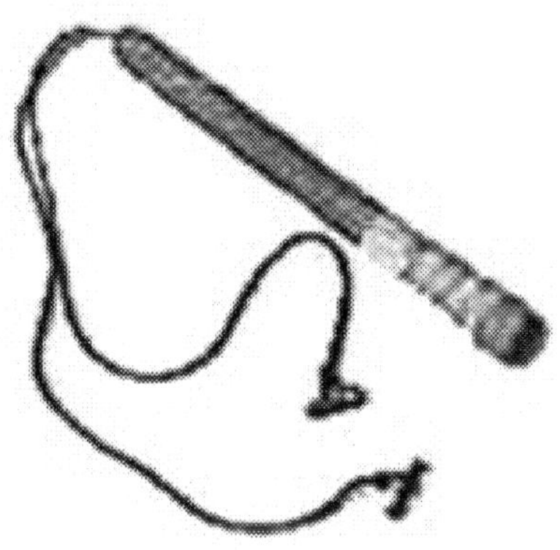

had to know that the crown of thorns, of which the Gospels speak, was an helmet shape and covered the entire head, not like the medieval crowns, but no one had this information because there was no historical memorial of it: the icons of the Passion present a Jesus with a crown like a ring and not with an helmet like the one which, how the experts affirm, produced the lesions to the head of the Man of the Shroud. It must also be noticed that the counterfeiter, if he existed, traced on the shoulders of the Man the abrasions of a beam and not that ones of a cross: he must have had uncovered, therefore, the prisoners came load, in order to go to their death, with the patibulum, one says the cross-sectional arm of the cross, not with the entire cross: the vertical arms of crosses were stablily fixed on the place of the execution, and those horizontal ones were added at the last moment, with the prisoner already attached to the patibulum by his own arms, by ropes or by nails like Jesus and other ones: he was killed in this way a certain John the *zelota*[3] whose remains were found in a tomb near

[3] The Hebrew zealots were rebellious partisans against the Roman occupants.

Jerusalem, and analyzed, in the year 1968. All the medieval images of the *Via Crucis* (still after and by now traditionally, because the Cross had become the symbol of the Passion) represent Christ who charges and transports on himself the entire Cross, like in the Middle Ages it was certainly believed. At last, the counterfeiter would have had to find a man with the same appearance of the Christ whose Face is painted on several Byzantine medieval icons made like the Shroud Face, and therefore, one may suppose, inspired to the same Shroud Face: the firsts, painted in Edessa, the others in Costantinopoli and in its empire and also in Italy: one may find these paintings, frescoes and mosaics in many Italian churches, like the *Christ Pantocrator* in the cathedral of Monreale in Sicily:

The first icons which was inspired to the Shroud Face are made in the VI century, age in which the Mandylion-Sindone was in Edessa. Before this period, Jesus was painted with several faces of the fantasy, one of them without beard and moustaches and with very short (and blond) hair, according to the hair cut of the nobles of Rome.

Knowing all these things, it's very difficult, or impossible, to think that a medieval counterfeiter indeed has existed.

54

Appendix 1

CHRONOLOGY

In the year/During the years

Events

April 7, year 30, Friday

Christ's Crucifixion and Death

April 8, year 30, Saturday, Hebrew Easter

Jesus in the grave, from the sunset of the previous day.

April 9, year 30, Sunday (it will become the Christian Easter)

Peter and John find the Jesus tomb open with inside his sepulchral flaxes. After few hours, Christ will appear revived to the Apostles.

From the 30 to the 524

There are various legends and no document. It's sure that, for the norms of purity of the Jewish (like the first Christians were), the burial linens are impure and they cannot be taken and never exposed. Therefore, if the two apostles have collected the Shroud (second another tradition, collected it the owner of the tomb, Joseph from Arimatea), it was hidden very well. Besides, like the cross is symbol of violent and shameful death, the Christians feel ashamed of the Cross until Vth - VIth centuries, when it begins to be the Christian symbol: before, there were the fish, the anchor, the boat and the anagram XP (in Greek letters; CR in Latin letters) that it was for Cristòs, Cristus (Christ).

525

The Holy Sophia church in Edessa is restored: opening a bulwark niche, it's found the image of a face of Christ on sheet, defined from the contemporaries "not made from human hand: acheropita". It's exposed framed and soon it's become an object of veneration. It's called popularly The Handkerchief (The *Mandilion*). The Byzantine iconography of the Sacred Face begins; the features of these icons are very similar to those of the Face of the Mandilion: according to studies carried out recently about icons from that period to the century XI, there are beyond 100 points of convergence, much more than the quantity demanded in a Court in order to establish that she is the same person. "Yes", you will say, "but what this matter has to do with the Shroud?". We will see about it.

944

The Byzantine empire conquers Edessa, town which had fallen in hand of the Turks, and asks for having the Mandilion. The Turks accept the request, even if for the Islam Jesus is one very important figure, because he is for the Muslims the prophet who immediately precedes and announces Mahomet (for the Christians, Christ, speaking about that Person, would have had intend the Holy Spirit descended on the Apostles in the day of Pentecost). The Mandilion is carried into Costantinopoli. One discovers that it is not a handkerchief but it's a shroud: it was exposed in Edessa refolded in eight parts and therefore only the Face remained visible. One may suppose that Christians and Muslims thought that it was not convenient to expose the image of the naked body of Christ and with all those wounds, excoriations and bruises that are on the Shroud Man. The Mandilion is therefore the Shroud, of which until the year 944 only the Face had become public. After, it's ostensa many and many times in Costantinopoli.

1204

During the Fourth Crusade the riders, controlled from Otto de la Roche, governor and duke of Athens, conquer Costantinopoli and, although the Pope had placed the prohibition, they steal many sacred images: the crusader Robert de Clary reports this fact in one of his relations. In the successive year, in a letter to Pope Innocent IV, a member of the Byzantine imperial family, Theodore Angel Comneno, asserts that a shroud has been stolen from Otto de the Roche and that this duke hides it in Athens. The sender asks the Pope to oblige Otto to give back the shroud because the Pope had given the order to do not depredate Costantinopoli. It's unknown if the Pope believed in the

letter, it's only sure that the Shroud (the one which is in Turin today?) did not go back into Costantinopoli; however it was never exposed from de la Roche, because the relics theft would have been punished with death, and the family had therefore the full interest to hide it and to worship it in their own house secretly.

1292 - 95

The Shroud may be found indirectly, it's on a miniature composed in the Pray Code in this period by an author who writes that he had seen a shroud and he paints it on the same Code; this shroud image presents some burns of a fire, it's unknown when it blazed, which are still today on the Shroud of Turin.

1314

A process is celebrated in France against the Templar knights and monks, upon the accusation of heresy, witchcraft and sodomy. The king Philip *The beautiful*, with such false imputation, wishes to confiscate (to steal) their immense treasures and to destroy their order which has become too powerful. The Great Master De Molay and other ones, between them Geoffroy de Charny (or de Charney like it's wrote in one of the reports of the process?) are condemned: they are burned on the rogue. They had been accused, among other things, to possess the image of a man with moustaches and beard who, according

to the accusers, would had been the representation of the demon Bafomet whom the condemned would had adore. It could be assumed to be the *Shroud of Turin*. There are historians (like the Englishman Jan Wilson: he was the first who thought and told it in 1976, during the pre-conference on the Shroud held in

Albuquerque) who have supposed that this Sheet had been stolen from Costantinopoli directly by the Templar knights (do not by the duke Otto de la Roche) and then the Shroud, after to have been seized to the templar de Charny (Charney?), had been donated from king Philip the Beautiful, towards the year 1350, to the homonym Geoffroy de Charny (may be his grandson or not a member of this family?). Moreover, there is no documentation about the fact the Order participated to the IV Crusade and I prefer to follow the hypothesis that the Templar monks do not have stolen the Shroud. It's curious to know that, many years after, between the relatives for wedding of the family de Charny there is a de la Roche, Umbert de the Roche, who is the husband of Daisy de Charny who is the last Shroud owner; in the year 1418, in order to avoid possible dangers to the Cloth, connected with the "War of the hundred years" which passes by in those years, he hides temporary the Shroud in Bourgogne, into the chapel of Buessard; but let's go a bit backward.

1353 - 56

Geoffreoy de Charny (perhaps the grandson of his previous homonym) in the year 1353 possesses the Shroud, this fact is attested by documents, in his own castle in own lands in Lirey. He promises to God that he will give the Shroud to the canon priests of Lirey if the France will gain the victory. The war is gained but he died during the battle; then his widow, who was born in the family Vergy, fulfils the husband's religious wow: in the year 1356 the document about this delivery to the canon priests is written: they have the Shroud and begin to oxtend it. It becomes very famous.

1356 - 1452

Peter d'Arcis (bishop of the diocese of Troyes in which the town of Lirey is) is an enemy of the Shroud which, without having see it, he considers certainly a painting image, made to trick the good faith of the Christian believers (but in effect, there are not pigment traces on the Shroud): he speaks and writes publicly against the Shroud. In these years there are arguments between the canon priests and the family de Charny about the rights on the Shroud; this Sheet is returned at last, definitively, to the original owners. All the passages of the Shroud from

the canon priests to the family and on the contrary are documented; between bracket: this means that Leonardo da Vinci, who will be born in the year 1452, isn't the Shroud maker.

1453

Daisy of Charny, who is the last heir of her family, by now widow donates (or she sells, because she's not anymore a rich woman) the Shroud to Anna of Lusignano, the wife of the duke of Savoy, Ludovico. From this moment, the Sheet resides in the capital of the Savoy, Chambery. A special chapel is constructed in order to honor it and guard it.

1532

There, in the night between the 3rd and 4th of December, a terrible fire bursts. The Shroud is saved at the price of serious burns of some priests. It's kept in a cowling and will be removed only two years after, at the presence of public notaries and of those who very well knew it and who attest, by a written report, that the damaged Shroud they have upon their eyes is certainly the same one. The suffered damages are transcribed: the principal ones are two parallels burnt lines and eight holes:

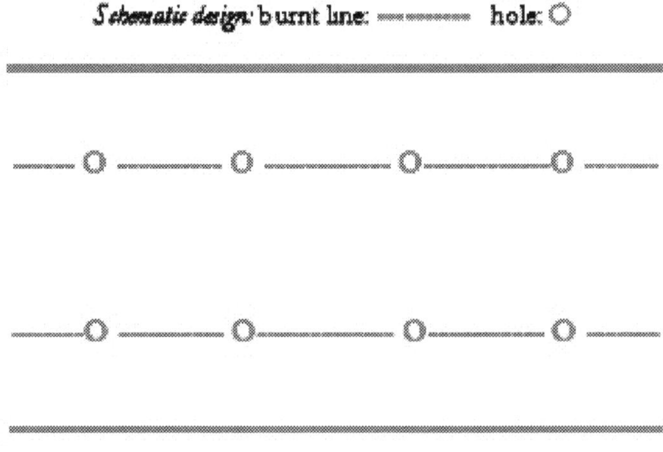

The opinion of an expert on the Shroud, Dr. Mario Cappi, that a drop of fused metal had been enough to make these damages: it was the pond which welded the outside of the wooden theca which guarded, folded in eight layers, the Shroud, to pierce them and to make those eight symmetrical holes. The Clare's nuns of the convent of Chambery were charged to make patches on the holes;

these patches remained on the Shroud until the year 2002; in order to reinforce the sheet, they sewed behind the Shroud, for all its amplitude, a cloth of Holland; in the summer of the year 2002, during jobs of restoration of the Shroud executed in Turin, the cloth has been removed, like the patches.

1572

Turin, where the Court of the dukes is moved, becomes the capital of the Ducat of Savoy.

1578

The duke Emanuele Filiberto (called "Iron Head") wishes to carry into Turin the Shroud, but the inhabitants of Chambery love and worship it and they want it to remain in their town. The occasion is given to the duke from a ballot of the archbishop of Milan, Carlo Borromeo: he had promised solemnly to go walking into Chambery for worshiping the Image of the Shroud, if the plague (one of the many plagues in these times) which infected Milan would have stopped in a hurry, and the plague suddenly ceased. The duke declares he wants to make the shorter for the archbishop who is not in very good health, and, by that excuse, he orders to carry temporarily the Shroud into Turin. It's received in Turin and put in the church called "Santa Maria *ad Presepe*", in front of the public square today named Castello (The Castle), near the Cathedral: this church will become only the chapel of the church of San Lorenzo, which will be planned by the great architect Guarini: a baroque masterpiece! In October, the archbishop reaches Turin. After his departure, the Shroud remains in Turin and it will never go back to Chambery.

Shroud Museum of Turin:
The container which was used in order to transfer the Shroud into Turin

1694

The Shroud, already guarded in the ducal palace, is transferred in a very beautiful chapel planned from the same architect who had designed the church of San Lorenzo, Guarino Guarini; this chapel is adjacent to the ducal palace from a part, and to the Cathedral from the other.

1706

Turin suffers the siege of the French army and the Shroud follows the dukes into Genoa. After the war, at the end of the same year, it is brought back to Turin.

1713

In this year the Ducat becomes a kingdom and it's the right occasion for one of the many much Oxtensions the Savoy family will made: in 1717 there is a second one, for celebrating the first four years of the kingdom.

1898

In occasion of the Oxtension in order to celebrate the wedding of the Prince Victor Emanuel, son of the king Umbert I and heir to the throne, Mr. Second Pia, attorney at law and very able amateur of photography, realizes, having the regal consent, the first photos of the Shroud: he declares, then, that the negative slab, as soon as developed, had almost fallen from his hand for the emotion, because he had uncovered that this negative slab was in reality a positive one regarding the image of the Man, and that all the rest, blood, patchs, burns, on the slab were normally negative. We are in the time of the atheist positivism, and many people accuse Mr. Pia of having deceived people good faith by photographic tricks. In reality, every photography released subsequently will carry to the same result.

1931

Oxtension for the wedding of Umbert, heir to the throne of Italy. New photographies of the Shroud (they are the more known ones), from part of Joseph Enrie, professional photographer.

1939

First Conference of Studies on the Shroud, in Turin.

1939 - 46

Because of the Second Worldwide War, in 1939 the Shroud is put to the shelter in the sanctuary of Montevergine (Avellino). It come back into Turin in 1946.

1969

The first coloured photos are made, by John Baptist Judica Cordiglia.

1973

Oxtension of the Shroud at the television sets, made by the Italian Radio-Television (RAI TV). In this occasion, a champion of the Shroud woven is captured and it will be analyzed, for the first time, by the *method of radiotatazione - C 14*, from Dr. Raes: disappointment of this scientist, because a part of the champion turns out of the year 200 and another one of the year 1000. Max Frey, University of Zurich, a botanist and a criminologist, captures on the Shroud, by adhesive tapes, some micro powders. He discovers, by the microscope, fossil pollens of some plants of Palestine, Anatolia and alpine zones.

1978

Oxtension in order to celebrate the 400 years from the transfer of the Shroud into Turin. From October 8th to 14th, many experts (in the greatest part they are American) analyze the Shroud during 120 hours without stopping, to the purpose of a multidisciplinary surveying.

1983

The former king of Italy Umberto II dies in Cascais, in Portugal; he was the owner of the Shroud and, in his testament, he has gifted it to the Pope John Paul II who arranges that the Shroud remains in Turin and, along the time, the caretakers are the archbishops of this town.

1988

Official experiments of *radiometric dating*.

1997

Fire in the Guarini's chapel. The Shroud is absent, guarded in Cathedral, because there are restoration jobs in the chapel. While the flames extend within the same Cathedral, Mr. Mario Trematore, fireman, with extraordinarily force cracks the antibullet theca guarding the Shroud and, with other firemen, he places it out. No damage for the Shroud.

1998

Oxtension from April 18th to June 14th, in order to celebrate the hundred years from the first photography of the Shroud.

2000

Oxtension from August 12th to October 22nd in occasion of the Saint Year.

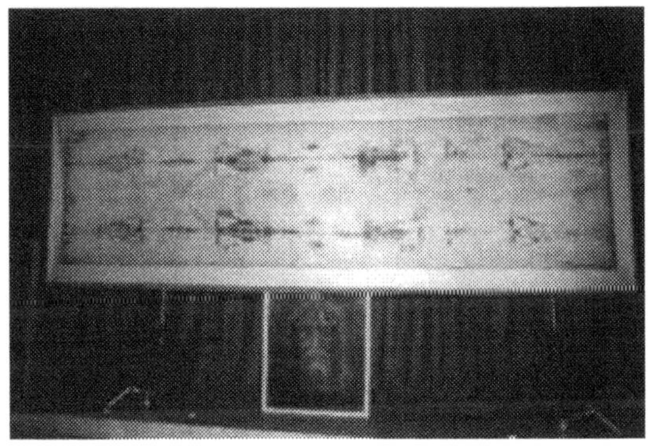

2002

Between June 20th and July 22nd the patchs and the cloth of Holland are removed from the Shroud. The jobs are made in the new sacristy of the Turin Cathedral, by some weave experts guided from the Swiss Dr. Mechtild Flury-Lemberg; between them, Dr. Irene Tomedi, Italian expert.

LA STAMPA

La Sindone cambia
Eliminati i rattoppi
vecchi di cinque secoli

Appendix 2

THE IMAGES WE FIND ON THE SHROUD

WOUNDS, LESIONS, BLOOD: THEY AGREE PERFECTLY WITH THE DESCRIPTIONS OF THE GOSPELS ABOUT THE JESUS CHRIST'S PASSION

Legenda

C: ! Zone of withdrawal of the samples

1 Wounds on the right foot

2 Water tracks (the water used against a fire?)

3 Wound in the chest side

4 Folds of the cloth

5 Beyond 120 scourge blows

6 Heel and plant of the right foot

7 Carbonized line of the fire

8 The patches on the cloth done by the Clare's nuns of Chambery (they have been taken away during the restorations in the summer 2002)

9 Bruises to the shoulders for the transport of the patibulum

10 Wounds to the nape caused from the "crown" (helmet) of thorns

11 Wounds on face and on brow

12 Wound on the left wrist

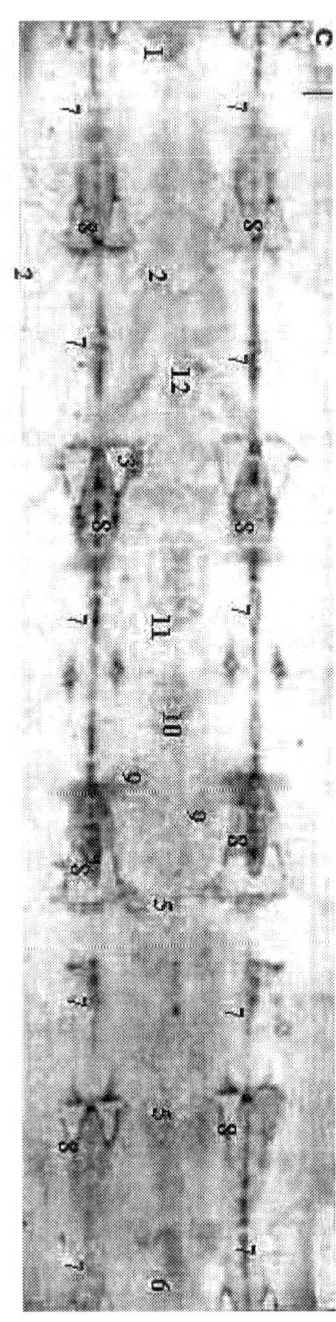
C
1
2
3
5
6
7
8
9
10
11
12

BIBLIOGRAPHY

The following writings of the conferences and the bibliographic books are in Italian language

1) Conferences during the years from 1998 to 2000 in the Saint Laurence Church of Turin, organized from the group of the volunteers for the Shroud Oxtension "Amici di San Lorenzo" (the relative writings are conserved in the secretariat of the same ones):

Medical team: Sindone (Shroud) e considerazioni di tanatologia. Il punto di vista della medicina legale.

Antonio Oddone, Chiacchierata sul Telo sindonico.

Antonio Oddone, Storia della Sacra Sindone.

Giovanni Latino, Perché la Sindone non può essere un falso.

Giovanni Latino, Apostolato attraverso la Shroud.

Giovanni Latino, Perché Gesù Cristo è stato condannato a morte in croce.

Aldo Guerreschi, La tridimensionalità sindonica ed il fotorilievo.

2) Publications:

a) <u>Newspapers:</u>

Federica Bello, Quell'impronta "alambicca-cervelli", in La Voce del Popolo, 20/8/2000

Francesca Paci, La Sindone cambia. Eliminati I rattoppi vecchi di cinque secoli, in La Stampa, 10/08/2002

b) Books:

Mario Cappi, La Shroud dall'A alla Z, Edizioni Messaggero.

Roberto di Clari (*Robert de Clary*), "La conquista di Costantinopoli": Studio critico, traduzione e note di Anna Maria Nada Patrone, Collana Storica di Fonti e Studi, Genova

Alfredo Orlando, Il punto sulla Shroud, ElleDiCi

Collana sulla "Sindone", serie di cinque volumetti, ElleDiCi

Geremia Dalla Nora, Il Volto di Gesù, ElleDiCi.

Vari saggi sulla Sindone di Pierluigi Baima Bollone.

Emanuela Marinelli, La Sindone - Un'impronta "impossibile", Ed. S. Paolo.

Aa.Vv., Sindone - "Il tuo Volto, Signore, io cerco" (Guida del pellegrino per l'Ostensione 2000), Edizioni San Massimo.

3) Internet:

http://sindone.torino.chiesacattolica.it

A SHORT BIOGRAPHY

Guido Pagliarino is a graduate of The University of Turin; his degree thesis was published by the Economic and Social History Institute of this University. The History of Economy and the History of Economic and Social Doctrines were very important for this author during his studies, under the guidance of Prof. Carlo Cipolla and Prof. Mario Abrate. In the following years, despite many wider interests, the Author's interest for history and philosophy has continued, above all about the Epistemology; in this interest, the discovery of books written by the philosopher K. R. Popper was very important: a discovery which has conduced Guido Pagliarino to come back to the Christianity. "The agnostic Prof. Popper's books?", one would question in astonishment. "Yes", is the Author's answer, "I was a positivist man, and by Karl Popper I opened myself to deeper and more humble searches". Prof. Poppers says, in substance, there is nothing certain in science; on the contrary, one can only temporarily accept a conjecture powered by experiments, and only if it is susceptible to be counterfeited. Then, Guido Pagliarino had thought: "Why should theology be treated any less than science?"; and he started researching on Christian history and doctrine. Intellectual meetings of a persistent, friendly association with Father Charles Jegge, until the death of that dear person, were the determining factor for the author's return to Christianity and for an ulterior deepening of his faith. The author has collaborated with many magazines; he has written for Talento (Talent), Controcampo (An Adverse Vision) Spiritualità e Letteratura (Spirituality and Literature), Vernice (Varnish), Penna d'Autore (The Author's Pen), Il Corriere di Roma

(The Rome Courier), Cultura e Società (Culture and Society) and Future Shock. This author has been honored with the "Award Of Culture By The Chairmanship Of The (Italian) Council Of Ministers" for his writings. Guido Pagliarino is author of novels and essays. Here, his last books (no one of them has been still translated from Italian into English):

Published by ***Prospettivaeditrice,*** *Civitavecchia, Roma, Italy*

- La vita eterna, saggio sull'immortalità tra Dio e l'uomo

2002, essay, ISBN 88-7418-106-X

- Gesú, nato nel 6 'a.C.' crocifisso nel 30

2003, essay, ISBN 88-7418-072-1

- Cristianesimo e Gnosticismo,

2003, essay, ISBN 88-7418-177-9

- Il giudice e le streghe

2006, novel, ISBN 978-88-7418-359-3

Published by ***Lulu Press,*** *Morrisville, NC, U.S.A.*

- Il Dio col grembiule

2006, essay, ISBN 978-1-84728-269-9

- The mysterious Shroud of Turin,

2006, essay, ISBN 978-1-84753-821-5

INDEX

ISBN-10: 1-84753-821-5

ISBN-13: 978-1-84753-821-5

First edition – October 2006

www.ingramcontent.com/pod-product-compliance
Ingram Content Group UK Ltd.
Pitfield, Milton Keynes, MK11 3LW, UK
UKHW041923190726
13854UKWH00003B/1400

9 781847 538215